Practicing for Heaven

Practicing for Heaven

Julia B. Levine

1998 Anhinga Prize for Poetry
Selected by Enid Shomer

ANHINGA PRESS, 1999
TALLAHASSEE, FLORIDA

*This publication is sponsored in part by a grant from the Florida
Department of State, Division of Cultural Affairs,
and the Florida Arts Council.*

Cover art: *Untitled* by Dana Freeman
Author photo: Steve Ekstrom

Cover design, book design and production by Lynne Knight

Library of Congress Cataloging-in-Publication Data

Practicing for Heaven by Julia B. Levine – First Edition

ISBN 0938078-62-3
Library of Congress Cataloging Card Number – 99-072404

Anhinga Press Inc. is a nonprofit corporation dedicated wholly
to the publication and appreciation of fine poetry.

For personal orders, catalogs and information write to:
Anhinga Press
P.O. Box 10595
Tallahassee, FL 32302
www.anhinga.org

Printed in the United States of America
First Edition, 1999

Acknowledgements

I am grateful to the editors of the following journals in which these poems (some in slightly different versions) first appeared:

Americas Review: "Fire," "Looking at Prokudin-Gorskii's
             Photographs for the Tsar"

The Bridge: Journal of Fiction and Poetry: "Indian Summer"

The Flatlander: "After reading that you have died," "Salmon Run
             on the Consumes River"

The Madison Review: "Deadlock"

The Nation: "My Gemini"

Nimrod: "Abduction Under the Hubble Telescope," "Angels,"
             "Baltimore," "Fontanelle," "Touching Wild Animals"

Prairie Schooner: "At the Vernal Pools," "Overdue"

Sky: "Nights on Lake Michigan"

Southern Poetry Review: "The Distance Apart from Her"

The Squaw Review: "When I no longer wanted to die,"

Zone 3: "Hunting Wild Mushrooms," "Why Numbers Never End"

I am also grateful to a fellowship from the California Council on the Arts, which helped fund the writing of several of these poems.

I especially want to thank my husband for his generous support and almost endless patience; my three children for sharing me; Ruth Schwartz, who, literally, made so much of this possible; Arthur Smith, for his support and kindness; my writer's group (Cynthia Bates, Jonathan Daunt, Susan Kelly-DeWitt and Hannah Stein), for their helpful criticism.

I also want to thank my friends, especially Amy Abramson, Nancy Aikin, Susan Brown, Susan and Randy Cohen-Byrne, Margie Ferguson, Patricia Floyd, Dana Freeman, Lisa Gottlieb, Gregory Humphreys, Adin Levine, Dawne Levine, Susan Shelton, and Charlotte Stombler, for their sustaining belief in me, my parents, Rhoda and Mark Levine, for introducing me to poetry as a child, and Elizabeth Pollie, for helping me survive in the first place. And finally, thank you to Enid Shomer for her careful and gracious reading of these poems.

For Steve

Contents

IV

Practicing for Heaven

" ... So it became
the world come

back to me   "

     — Anita Barrows
      So It Became

I

Walking Beside the American River

Water spreads a flat pewter between cottonwoods.
And though the sun is strangely gentle,
the children and you shirtless in a warm wind,
I cannot forget how the past is just behind us.
I remember the doctor touching my arm,
as if the bad news needed a place to enter,
while outside that window, a field of sunflowers
shimmered in their yellow blaze. I saw then
death was a tearing apart
from all that did not stop, and nothing,
not even the lilies in a red glass
trembling as the nurses came and went,
or the stubborn grace of our children
hurling themselves over the hospital lawn,
could seal that sudden looming
between this world
and where you had almost gone. So that now,
when each thing is newly returned,
it is more difficult to turn away
from the water's glistening sweep,
to let the least hour drift out of reach
without wading into this river.
We each carry a child close against us,
and thigh deep in the gliding darkness,
this is another way to know
the current pulls hard
against our holding on.

Vigil in Cherry Season

In the repeated heat of June,
I read about a Buddhist nun
tortured, imprisoned below ground
and there, in captivity, how she learned
the most about patience and faith,

so, in the next weeks,
when dread kept me hard strung
beside what was still alive in you,
the neon pulse of machines
watching over the failing choir of your organs,
I thought of that nun in darkness,
and the light she carried
as a persistent burning to be changed.

I wanted the past to stop hurting me
with the sting of sunned metal
as we lifted the ladders into the cherry tree,
with the numinous hours before your collapse
when I sat on the garden steps
tearing apart the small globes,
slipping out the stone pits,

and in the hushed night of the hospital,
I laid my head into your listless hand.
I saw my fingers still inked red,
and the scratch on your arm
from the whip of a branch. I thought then
of those cherries as candles,
and my hands dipped into the burning colors
of the sensate world.

And I thought of the nun
marching round the Chinese square,
flinching as the ordained were shot by soldiers,
and I saw her saffron-robed and glimmering,
walking into a trusted unknown.
How had she remained floating
above the tangible, not even looking back
as each thing moved deeper
into the heart of the world? I was so stained

with all you had sweetened in me,
that even when it was certain you would return,
and I could almost understand
the ghostly language of faith
as an argument with pain,
I stayed bent over your body for hours,
as if warming myself with matter,
as if listening to your dying
settle its stony dark back inside.

Fourth of July

Lisp of dried grass
down to the revelation of water,
where even the heat eases
and a dimming light
oils your shoulders. We sit in Cache Creek,
each of us holding a child in our arms,
letting their bodies
fly over the fast running, and everywhere we turn,

I see barely healed scars
in the musculature of the sky, the places
anyone might leave this world forever. Finally,
it seems, I have learned nothing
from how close you came to dying,
except that whatever carried you back to me
did not need to love each small thing
as if it would be lost.

A cloud of bees
has gathered to drink from shore
and as we rub the children dry,
their hovering rises and settles
with the wings of our towels. And even later,
when we lie on blankets,
watching the sky flare with gunpowder,
each thudding burst of color
followed by the children's gasping joy,

it is the lingering after falling light
I see: it is the urgency of darkness
that rises and folds over each brief flare;
it is every path the burning has taken
that suddenly blackens and is gone.

Why Numbers Never End

We walked to water through a field of star thistle,
spores shivering in wind.
She was counting as high as she could,
while my hands lifted a blaze of hair from her lips.
I was thinking how my quarry of genes
laddered her legs and arms,

as we kneeled in the river's muck,
watching knots of minnows and tadpoles
interrupt the shadows. She was four years old
when she asked me why the numbers never end.
And I didn't know why
perfection allows us near enough to grieve.
I only knew that the wholeness of her world
was about to change.

So I said, *Look at the river,*
and she saw water
endlessly counting itself over stones
and the blue, blue hills.

Abduction Under the Hubble Telescope

After they find her body, her face remains on the billboard
I drive past each day, like music
lingering after the damper has fallen.
How familiar her smile
taut with secrets she can barely contain,
waking from the inside out.
And knowing that dark hair, parted on the side,
how it spills over her shoulders,
I am like any parent
forever turning around a child's picture,
even after she has burned her way
into something else. Above me, a hovering light

marks two men floating in that night sky,
devoting themselves to such small repairs
with hands made enormous from error,
their bodies helplessly bumping away
from the feeble signals of reason and science.
If only they could focus deeper into the window
he took her through, open the round hills of that dairy farm
where her heart was stopped down. Instead

the bleating red of their ship
hurtles through miles of silence, so far above
Christmas lights winking from the neighbors' rooflines,
our mulberry wept clean of leaves, and my daughter
asking if God wants us back.
How clumsily we love this world:
looking into that vast darkness,
waiting for the telescope
to send down unseen colors of light.

— *in memory of Polly Klaas*

Where We Sleep

All day, the sun is hushed as moon.
We walk through fog
as if the fields were skating, each clouded thistle
gliding into the place we have just entered.
Later, you draw a fire,
your hands hard with brick and weather.
When you first came home from the hospital,
how I loved most
your shoes newly returned to the hall, your shirt
thrown to the floor, the house changed
by what the living go on doing.
I remember too, a welling up of heat
in the porch steps at dusk, an empire
hinted at in each warm tomato
twisted from the vine. I listened carefully, then.
And for days, hearing you speak
was a window
into whatever room you already slept inside.

Now I turn the dark coals back to flame.
All night, the fog will come close as it can.
I move my hand through your hair.
I tell myself, we are not silent,
but spoken through.
I say, *Wait,*
knowing winter is merciful
and my unopened grief
nestles deep as seed. Oh, I would say anything
not to leave this room just yet.

In Spring

1

Seven days the blackness rises
into white, a hovering like snow
over the Capay valley,
almond orchards deep in bloom.

Already trees drift bare.
My children run the mown trail,
shaking every dark branch
they can reach. I walk behind them,
thinking of innocence
as this impossible sweetness

and my wonder as a punishing vigil,
an exceeding of expectation
beside all that must fail.

Driving home, we pass a roadkilled possum
and my youngest asks,
Do you think he was crying?
The older one tells her,
Winter is sad because so much has to die.
See *that grass*, she says, *see that tree*,

and I look
at a handful of swallows thrown into sky,
at tiny torches of mustard
scattering light through these fields,
at this beauty
visiting so briefly it can only hurt.

2

Dressing the children for Purim, I slip gold bracelets
over their wrists, while a strange silence
follows gusts of wind. The tornado watch
has not yet been announced,
and the newspaper, thrown to the far side of our porch,
is still folded around a picture of Israeli police
laying the stained gowns of so many Esthers
into the street, drawing blankets over small arms
sequined with glass and nails, holding back a crowd
from the bomber's remains.

And though omen is what resonates
long after the hour has ended,
and I am listening miles past these fields,
it is not until we return from the carnival,
– after I have watched my daughters'
perfect faith in plenty,
how they steady breath and line
enough to snag pennies from a pool –
that I understand fate
as whatever loss I am about to hold
while they go on, unaware
that sometimes we are saved
and sometimes we are not.

3

His father burned the boy's stomach on a radiator,
so for days the staff peel bandages from his skin,
trembling when he cries, frightened
by the yellow work of his healing. And the girl
whose infant sister was shaken until she died,
is nearly mute, no questions about her mother,
no answers for anything we say. In my office
at the Emergency Shelter, I ask little,
having learned the body remembers best.
So the boy scissors the curtains,
buries bread under his mattress, while the girl
tosses children down dollhouse stairs,
and startled by a distant car, trembles,
turning not just her eyes, but her entire life

away from me. Then, a month after she arrives,
the girl asks me for markers and paper.
She wonders if I have ever wanted to rewind time,
answering before I can, that wishing stars
are only a way into dreams
you must finally wake from. *Nothing will ever come true,*
she says, drawing her dead sister in the clouds.
She has wings now
because she wants to follow me around.

4

On my way home, I park beside a creek.
Plumes of quince and cherry
shiver in a North wind. Sometimes
I grow so tired of loving this world,
that I think of death as a canoe
finally shored, and my soul
asleep in new grass,
no longer greedy
for the music of a child
walking through a stream,
dipping her hands in black mud,
asking *Why can't we stay here forever?*

5

And still I cannot help myself thinking,
How beautiful they are
in this swept-apart sky,

the lush banks of iris

brushed through with wind,
while a hard dark
gathers under these clouds.

Oh, to be given
the chance to begin again! For days
I have been entering the garden

expecting tattered husks,
and instead
there are blue epistolaries

impossibly tigered and revealed,
sending up
their startling azure. So much

trembles inside this spring,
that today when the tulips broke open
their red cups to sun,

I knew the wound was everything,

and the heart is that moment
of being torn-apart, that terror
unsealed and blooming.

Strand Line

It is almost dusk
when we enter the rocky dark of a riverbed.
Here, between tiny stars of moss,
I wonder how it would be to love
what I have been given
and ask for nothing more.
It is late in November.
We have talked for weeks and always
the same two answers arrive.
Yes and no. Keep her. Do not.
Listen, even if I was certain
I wanted the child I am carrying,
the heart is only a brief light
worrying shadow,
and each interval out of darkness
climbs through a torn shape
aching to be restored,
and the soul
asking to be let go.
Now we follow the creekbed higher.
When we reach Island Lake,
it is too late to see
the intricate scrawl of coves,
or the currents changed by wind.
But in this near blackness
I can hear into the silence of granite.
Venus rises over the hard shore of sky,
while the water slows to grey.
Seven woodducks rush skyward,
crying as they leave us behind
on the strand line of every moment.

Angels

A strange barking sounds from the long mast of geese.
How slow the forest in winter, all day
only a handful of dead branches
falling gently down
around this lake. And how fairly snow
seeks out the bones of each pine,
spanning across the uneven ground like sleep,
while something hovers just beyond sensation.

This stillness
must be a kind of music:
a couple staring out at sun
burning from the basin's rim,
the young woman
letting newspaper float from her hands,
a dog turning back
where the pier has buckled. It has been several months

since the catamarans swelled with wind, a moment
suddenly drawing me forward
into the question of God.

Then I did not know
grief can only learn a shoreline.

And I had not yet seen
this sky entering each black-winged bird
as it climbed out of dark water
into the mercy of so much light.

My Gemini

Because she is waiting to be lifted
out of the silence of my unremembered life,
nothing can rinse her from what I carry
or how I travel these fields,
watching magpies scatter arrows into the sky,
and always knowing she slipped apart
from what was once seamless,
so that something of me, though torn,

would keep on arriving. Ahead of me
combines are spinning knives
deep into the ground,
leaving combs of threshed hay
to argue for a world that cuts everywhere.

This is how she wants me to walk,
steady and awake, into all that dies
before it can return, the last leaves
whispering further and further into silence,
these thistles bony with light,
and only the ravens black enough
to spill over with such a thin sun.

She wants me to touch it all,
knees bent in asters,
my fingers rattling petals,
remembering the months
she wrapped my mittened hand
back around the spoon, urging me to dig
down to the tiny locket
netted in the roots of our sugar maple.

She wants me to know even darkness
will speak if you listen, that each hidden word
asks to come to light,
that someday my body will call for her
to step back in.

Until then, she says,
we are practicing for heaven,
and this is how you get there,
the ladder built rung by rung
with the truth of whatever happens.

II

Touching Wild Animals

Somewhere winter is arguing for another country,
hills collapsing into a slate sky,
dimension wandering away in a flurry of crystal,
and a sly light greases the forking plows

as a child looks to lose count of the way home.
If she can walk outside her father's language,
the deer will recognize her grace,
the red fox will hear how faith and danger

circle her chest uneasily. She brings bread
but never puts it down, devotion
still the most secret place within. And everywhere
she tries to dissolve into perfect silence,

wind sends the saplings into her. Years
she waits, erasing the angels her arms
sweep across the white forest, breathing heat,
then ash into her scarf, even as she startles

to see snow fall in so many ways,
– stark white of egrets blazing from fields,
confetti of gulls undone from the sea.
Even here in this valley

where the untouched have no season,
winter hurrying color with rain,
still it is not over,
her own children crouching, silent

beside this pond of wild geese, their patience
a memory of the garden opening,
field of songbirds, rabbits, even wolverines
so close, her hands bristle.

Fire

The horse knows the sky is bitter with ash;
you can see the tremble in his graze,
how he startles his forelegs against the trough
before dipping down to water.
But horses know nothing of regret,

of the vast distance between this fire
burning down the hills and my brother
jumping the creek with me to crouch in thistles,
launching sparks over the railroad ties into farmland,
watching each ember lift like a seeding light.
How close to sin I was then,
the missed lick of flame that might have drawn
a farmer rushing to the paddock, his face
ruddy with heat and terror, throwing latches,
slapping cows apart, standing back
as animals thundered down the stalls.

Now the horse shadows me as I walk the fenceline,
the way the past keeps us in sight as we move ahead,
and I remember my father
groaning as he bends to the swastika
singed into our lawn, rubs his eyes with a handkerchief.
And later when he enters with a boy
I barely know, I listen at the study door.
In one hand, my father holds a glass of water.
He is drawing his other hand
across a map of the Russian Pale
into the complicated geography of exile.

He wants the boy to understand prayer
as water filling any shape that is offered,
and that fire, though it begins with so little,
must finally ask for everything.

The Girl I was Saving

The blue of my Sunday dress was dark as night
and if it was a good moon,
and my father turned away from my door,
singing his pocket of coins onto the dresser,
coiling his stethoscope over the hook,
I would remember the rabbi
and the strong wood of the bench
smooth against my back. *Blessed are you going in,*
and blessed are you going out, he chanted
as the children laid their ribbons down
into the seam of our prayer books. Then,
I wondered if God knew something
my father did not. My father always said
I would never be loved, and every night
that he cursed my face with his hands,
I was broken deeper from holy.
But in winter, when I crouched
under our seven pines,
watching chickadees hop across
the sorrow of our crusted lawn
without falling through,
I could believe this world
was where someone might wait for help.
Because even if I were blessed going in,
I needed to know how to stay hidden
until the dying summoned my father out.
And even if prayer was a chance
that mercy might find my house,
listening to those small spaces
between heaven and earth
was how the stillness learned to hold me,
like snow, like the black cage of maples
touching against silence,
like that torn canoe of moon,
unhinged and floating.

Nights on Lake Michigan

Downstairs, bitter voices wolved my door
and listening pulled the terror closer

until my room swelled with grim animals
stalking the forest around our cabin:

porcupines rasping bark off porch railings,
bats spitting darkness across the sleeping elms.

What child could have made another dream
from the bones of that cabin? At my window,

the lake soured into blackness. No moon yet.
If only I could have seen a path winding into morning

the way our rolling dock would stretch into the lake,
away from where my parents simmered in lounge chairs,

my mother tying up laces on three pairs of shoes,
my father devouring journals of disease,

his ear tuned to the peculiar music of the body's
pipes and strings. A path that would have led away

to where water held me as if my weight were sweet
and the underwater sand were rice paper

printed with tiny shells; away to where the wind rose up
as if someone called from the further shore,

whitecaps repeating my lost name. If only night
had been a smaller lake I could swim across,

where nightjars gently celloed in the rushes,
and sleep was how the silence borrowed me.

At Fourteen

Again the darkness that is rain,
gloomy mouths of gutters, rings in puddles
opening like half-starved chicks,
and except for the afternoon
Richard takes me home from school,
– his Buick like a crusader's boat
plowing through the downtown streets –
I work hard against my life,
carve initials in my wrist,
grimace as the blade point turns.
I am learning pain can be a mother;
pain can tell you *think again,*
but Richard, at seventeen,
three months from skipping town,
is generous with what he does not need to keep,
and so he's kind, says *Put on your nightgown*
while he undresses down to shorts
and climbs into my bed. All night
the river has been rising, and across the tracks
cows are bawling in the flooded barns,
sloughs erasing banks, willows midtrunk
in a raging pond. This moment, though,
is where my luck flips right side up
and Richard lies down inside my life forever,
how he holds apart the sheets
and takes nothing but the weight of me
onto his chest, black sworls of hair
as if a current had just run by,
his nipples flat and smooth as stones,
the astonishing closeness of his ear
when I whisper *Richard,*
and he groans awake. I follow him
far as the screened-in porch.
Rain fills the empty runnel of my street

with sky, poor shelter of the branches
softened.
Soon he'll drive out of state
and drink until he's dead,
his windows clouded as the Buick pulls away,
his hand raised or not, it almost doesn't matter.

— in memory of R.B. 1955-1998

Afterward

we jimmied open his window
and leapt into the rushes, that breathless cold
parted by our sudden, forgiven weight.
When he pulled me to his chest,
I dangled over the murky bottom,
and the water did not rinse, but returned us
to the hours in his room, his fingers,
my mouth, fervent pace of our thighs
softening in that humid spill of noon.
So, long before the night my father found my empty bed,
and refused to let me in the house,
before that dawn I crawled from under our pine,
and looked up at a robin, balanced on the furthest branch,
already I knew something about rising up,
already I had the lucky bullseye of that pond
holding me in the beginning of someone else's hands.
My brother and sister had unlocked the door.
I remember them at the kitchen table
in their pajamas, frightened and unmoving,
cereal boxes tall beside them,
the milk not yet poured, my heart thudding
as I banged out once again
to the corner where I waited
for his motorcycle to sputter and cut.
I had learned to wrap my legs around his
so the hot chrome would not blister my shins,
to lean into the highways' curves,
until it seemed we could be righted
only by willing ourselves to fall. It was July
and I had just turned sixteen
when he uncrossed the common brown of my arms
to whiteness underneath. And it was the first time
I belonged to something that did not hurt,
a moment when I was so much wanted
it seemed the marsh had chosen me –
deerflies lighting on my shoulders
minnows swarming my paddled feet,
a turtle nibbling gently at my circled arms,
my tangled, floating hair.

Looking at Prokudin-Gorskii's
Photographs for the Tsar

After the first rain, the almost breath of decay
rises from the lawn. All week, strange with fever,
I dreamt of my Russian aunts in bathrobes
standing in half-sleep at the sink,
circling their hands over plates
to summon a distant light into the kitchen,

and as the sickness learned what it could of my body,
my muscles roped and then undone,
I saw we are often pointed in a dark direction,
only to make that sudden turn back home. Today,
sitting in the garden, turning these pages
through a country tempered for the Tsar,

the world seems changed,
the earth deep with yellowed leaves, the sun
dimming and faded. Finches move restlessly
through the bare house of our rosebush.
Of course, there are no pictures of the White Pale.
But reaching out from all that will never be seen:

a photograph of a Ukrainian peasant.
She looks out at the ribbed clouds
of a vast sky, stern and yet afraid, as if watching
what had arrived to press her ghostlike
into the sparse grass.
Around her are thorns of locust trees,

the frame of a split corral. And because
there are no pictures of the hunted people
my grandparents buried in Prussian forests,
I look long at her instead,
imagining the moment the camera blazed,
the air bitten with sparks. I see her

at twenty, poured through with such heat
that it seems she flares from inside
with all the past cannot hold,
believing she will always be more
than a faint stain on darkness, trusting light
to never turn anyone away.

Hunting Wild Mushrooms

When he tracks the wild spores,
probing the underside of oak
for orange trumpets of Chanterelle
or the inky blush of Bluetts,
centuries of mycelium strands
threading the forest floor, waiting for weather
to lift the fruiting bodies out of blackness,

I think of what sliver of chance opened
in the years before war,
his parents crossing the Atlantic with linens
and the wedding pictures where they sit
on a narrow bench among ghosts:
stern aunts, a blonde child straddling shoulders,
young men still flush with dance and vodka,
entire families about to button up those dark coats
of earth, the soldiers' rifles insistent
that they dig their own graves
by handfuls, a village of bodies
sinking under the forest's dense litter;

so that now, when he kneels in the greying canopy
exhuming Amanitas, I see his hands
as prayer, how they reveal to light
what waits to be remembered,
their search
for what returns from that damp quiet.

The winter he left

there was no rain,
the air heavy
with unwept clouds,
the sky mostly fallen
over the walnut orchard,
and all that marked a row
inside those stubbled fields,
dissolving into fog.
                    Each dusk,
I stood at my office window,
staring at the dull horizon
bruised and fading.
I ran my hands through the sandtray
where children lost
what they wanted to find. Sometimes
my fingers suprised a buried stone
or a tiny angel,
and rubbing it clean,
I tried to return the figure to the story,
the one where he told me
there was no one else,
or later, how a man stood on our porch
holding out my husband's letters to his wife.
            Always there was that moment
turning off the light,
a glimpse of two chairs facing each other,
emptied and flashing back to shadow,
the sound of my shoes on gravel,
the way the road heaved and blurred
until I had to pull onto the shoulder
and turn the radio loud to weep.
            I cried in every room
of our house, kneeling on the pantry floor,
face down beside the sofa,
my forehead cold
against the plumbing of a sink.
I walked after dark

looking for a light in his rented room,
but most times,
even that was gone.
    Hard to say, then,
exactly how misery rinsed me clean,
why one morning
the drowning white of our bed
woke me, linen and calm,
and stepping onto the balcony
I was given back
one minute at a time
to the sun in March,
the first plum blossoms
beginning to unfold.
    Joy was a splinter
I felt as it entered,
while warmth slanted between the rails,
and a hummingbird pulsed
close enough to drink.
I sat with my hand to myself,
the weak sun on my thighs,
a rich briefness of scent,
     almost animal,
how I knew to help the wound
that way, over and over,
palm to touch, to heal.

First Day of the New Year

The same protests of light
against my window, the same oranges
lingering inside a darkened tree.
It seems nothing begins
with a broomhandle clothed in my hand,
dust rising in the pause between floorboards,
and yet the world comes down to us
when we are most anchored. Today,

watching an egret flying low over these fields,
I remembered a slow afternoon like this
when the monterey pines shivered with wind,
and my hands rested in the lake of his sink.
Then I did not know my faith
in repeated pleasures,
or how each moment waits to be split apart
by all that wants to enter.

And when he sat me at the table,
his garden just outside the glass doors,
the slide of plum clenching cold into a bud,
so much was already opening
where his voice
walked backwards into silence.

I remember waiting in that kitchen
for what could be turned back,
but there was only the clatter of a passing train,
the rails swift with light
binding sky to another journey.

So even as the door returned without him,
the whole of that beloved world
closing down around me,
I heard the lyric of every hour
carried always further,
and I felt each rumbling instant
taking its cargo deeper into history.

Driving Through Montana

Miles of pine leaned into sky,
thousands of luminous flies
streaming against the darkness
and that endless yellow line.

It was deadly serious,
how we drove so fast,
a box of crackers in my lap
and his hand inside my thigh
each time he wanted more.

From this distance,
memory seems like music
how the best parts are repeated –

his hair matted with dust and pine litter,
the stamping of wild horses
outside our tent, the silence
before he'd crumble down and cry.

Some promises take a long time to forget.

One night, there was a woman
walking that road alone,
her breath smoking in the cold,
her mouth split and bleeding,
and when we stopped for her.
she mumbled, joking, I think,
Do you mind if I sing along?

And what could it hurt
to pretend the world is music,
and damage is just the silence
that makes the rest a melody.

From this distance,
almost nothing looks broken.

III

Overdue

Alone with this songless waiting, body and sky
know what they must, and leave me outside
listening in, while our stove
grinds endlessly through stacks of wood,
and a great heron lifting from the pines
calls me into fields rutted hard with ice.

There, behind the barn, where horses snort from dark stalls
and crows burn themselves like charcoal embers
into leafless oaks, I unlatch the strangely mute hives,
and discover months of dismantling:
red mites gnawing architecture into dust,
ants gorging on stores of honey, nine generations of bees
shriveled into handfuls of pollen. There is another calendar

where all afternoons orbit around a heart stopping,
the last drone dragging himself into silence. And if I believe
that the universe is bodiless, the hive emptied
so something else can begin, then
Lord, let it be tonight:

a full moon awakening our window,
raising me up like a woman schooled in prayer
to what cannot be explained or understood
but simply lifted into my arms. After all the unnoticed hours,
to have this one moment

when, still rooted with cord, her breath first unfolds
from the body's accordion that will be her life.

Fontanelle

1.

Stranded in that clockless month of her arrival,
I listen to our neighbor sawing down back doors,
and rock her, tiny fists of breath uncurling,
while the details of each afternoon are revealed:
that still hour before the mailman crosses the street
to unlock his grey tomb of letters, or after school,
children looking for a game to start, and finally
scarlet lights weeding the horizon,
when the men silence their tools and only darkness
bangs out across the empty lots. Now the homeless women
are shaking olives from roadside trees, black pellets
raining down on their plastic bonnets
as this room gathers us into the heart of the house.
Torn up from sleep,
without a memory of dreams, all that will remain
in the essential loneliness before dawn,
is blue milk running from my body
and the violence of her genderless desire
clamping down on my skin.

2.

And then as I stare mutely out the window
at the shut door of the world, there is a night of weather,
trails of light scarring blackness, pelting whip of rain
rattling the fenceline. As giant conifers
crack and fall in the cemetery, the dead around us
unable to hold onto that last tangled handful of roots,
I begin my journey through each child's room,
knowing I am not tending their fear, but my own,
that I will never again travel far enough away
to be injured, to feel wilderness jar against me.
I count the miles between lightning and thunder
as the distance narrows and then widens in retreat.
And when I return to summon you up from sleep,
how desperately I want that brief moment of overlap:
when what was seen can finally be felt, that brilliant flash
when the self finally marries what it was
with what it has become.

3.

As she begins to arrive within her body,
I dare touch the fontanelle,
a vein visibly pulsing under that taut canvas,
tiny plates of skull still undone. Outside,
empty songs of the builders' hammers
flush a handful of crows into the sky. All winter
between rains searing streets into rivers,
sandbags packed around the sewer's roaring throat,
workmen waited inside steamy cabs of their trucks
to forge that blue carbon into a neighborhood.
Now when I take her out among the dark scars
of newly rolled streets, sidewalks not yet lined
with chalk drawings or paired initials,
her eyes without vocabulary,
a hare bounds out ahead of us,
dark-tipped ears sliding between wall guides
of new houses that stand open, without secrets,
a forest of forms not yet fully seen:
the world just before it can be known.

Rio Vista

Wind everywhere, the sound of grasses
struggling to be unfastened, the sound of the world
falling in love with emptiness.
When the baby would not stop crying,
we laid her down, and ran, laughing,
a terrible joy to be loosened of her.
The trail ended at the spit, a thin lapping of sand
before the estuary fingered into two creeks.
A ghost moon was about to flower.
I turned back.
She was silent where we had left her
under a shuddered elm,
staring up at the wildly tossing leaves.
And all the way home,
past orchards belled with pears,
the brack slowly pouring into darkness,
a great heron unfolding into flight,
I watched the lights breaking on water,
and thought, for the first time,
of the hidden weight of sky
only a lifted wing can reveal, how
without memory, we would be set adrift,
moorless, nothing to shape or hold us true.
And I saw too, it was her fearless gaze
that frightened me most, that she belonged
more to the bridge we were crossing,
than to the opposing summons
of either world, hovering as she did
just outside our past,
so that it was possible to feel,
even briefly, buried in a future
without her, while the moment flooded open,
the thrumming wetlands swollen with dusk,
moonlight rimmed and spilling,
so much to carry, that I knew then
this was abundance, this grief beside us
for all we would drop along the way.

Before Language Speaks the Loss

She climbs bearlike up the slide,
foot to palm over sunwarmed tin.
In the distance,
seven sprinklers arc over the green,
white plumes turning together
and apart.
A dark bird
flies over their shining,
the way a streak of bad luck
outlines happiness.
This morning,
she sat up from my arms
and fell backwards,
believing everywhere rises to hold her.
Is that how it feels to fly,
to plunge through gravity's want
into self-desire,
wordless and whole?
Now she wants to walk in circles,
her hands wrapped
around my index fingers,
her feet tilted on toe
as if in dance.
Behind us, the spigots pulse,
seven fingers hushing seven mouths,
the noise I make
as we sit under an elm
and she lies back into me,
her body as cloud,
and the sky in how she lets go,
her untouched silence as longing
asleep in the entire lake of mine.

Baltimore

She sings as we climb these hotel stairs, the moon rising
above all the sadness she cannot imagine:
two boys scraping windshields at a stoplight,
whine of sirens rushing to the endpoint of despair.

                              Though it is unlikely
she will remember tonight, chasing fireflies over lawns,
the air oiled with what rain makes of light,
I hold so tightly to all of these days
when she is still young enough to heal us –
when watching her cup the iridescent beetle
I can witness how faith transforms the world,
green coal pulsing in the awe of her palm.

Now we enter this strange room
the way she enters each day, without habit,
or the tarnish time wears into place.
She wilts into the tugging, arms barely aloft
as I drag a stained shirt over her head,
all the melody whispering from her untouched body.
All the barren, unlived hours before she arrived
fall from the starched sheet
I draw over her, gently
folding her limp arm back onto the bed.

                              Oh the joy of belief
that can withstand collapsing this deep.

By Heart

In school, my oldest child learns
the facts I have mislaid. *Birds sing
to mark their territory*, she says.
Each bird, a different song.
I am nursing the baby
as I listen, imagining the moment of birth,
sudden machine of breath and blood
bursting into perfect rhythm
without rehearsal. *On the moon,*

we would all weigh the same.
she says, working the numbers that row out
in counted lanes, the certain wealth of 8 times 8,
vast plains of longing tabled, and for now,
what can argue with all these lost hours
entering deeper into afternoon,

with the words she copies
from her spelling list: *Rose, snow, flying.*
I study her, as if listening
to the silent letter of her soul
travel back through language
into that moment before longing
shapes a life.

This is memory, then, at the beginning,
a child deep inside the present,
a world not yet learned by heart,
and her future still unharmed,
arriving out of the past
we will stand inside,

so that those she needs most
stand for her against grief, against loss,
stand the way birds sing
to defend the borders
they believe they own.

The Distance Apart from Her

1.

The fruit trees had already given up
their clouds of blossom,
the white so starry and fast, everywhere I turned
fog was folding back
around the small heat of violets and peonies. Driving home
we stopped to watch the rancher's colts,
clumsy with joy, kicking and bolting in circles,
the fields clenched in such a tender green.
But in her room, she would not lift her dolls
past their relentless silence into play.
Mama? she would begin,
trailing me into the kitchen, as I lifted lids,
turned from the steam, and
when I stopped my knife,
set the carrots like unlit candles
back onto the wooden board,
she answered, *Nothing.*
Crying, she seemed so small
to have so much dragged down
by the unfinished weight of grief.

2.

The weather was undecided and lifted
a luminescence up and down over our yard.
One sealed tulip was breaking red into light,
and I was listening to a freight train
groan through a country of doorways,
a tribe of women
pinning white sheets like vowels
to the vast mouth of this delta.
So why did suffering want this house, this room,
this child? I remembered myself as a girl,
dressed in a nightgown. How every winter,
our sleeper car tunneled under Lake Huron
into Canada, rumbling through the mysterious darkness
of all that had been done
or not done enough.
And waking on that train,
while my sister slept beside me,
I would press my nose against the window
and wait,
the sudden flare of a lit house
rushing towards me
out of everywhere I had not yet been.

3.

Because my mother had never placed me inside history,
there were no original names to call forward,
no one to take us over the dark wood floors
where my grandmothers must have kneeled,
not daring to look up, not wanting to feel
rough hands notice what the woolens hid.
I knew it had taken years
to walk the Polish forests, years working
the English rail to earn passage,
and finally, months of foul meat and bad seas
to reach this room, where I now sat,
washing the birdfine bones of her chest,
listening to the music of my cloth
pulling through water. Unraveling her braids,
unbuttoning her blouse, I had tried to invent
the world behind me: a wooden row house,
two plump mothers cross-stitching a tablecloth,
a boy crawling through the henhouse for eggs,
the girl that was my grandmother
staring at the soldiers' sabers
as her father stopped begging for mercy
and died at the bottom of their well, leaving her
with nothing but a wordless murmuring
to pour into the strange momentum
that was the carrying forward,
that was my own child.

4.

Late at night,
when the tule fog would return,
erasing the houses into ghost script,
streetlamps leaking yellow,
fences blurred into dust,
I saw how easily we could disappear.
She was sleeping under a fury of blankets,
toy horses set carefully around the bed,
a closet of shoes, emptied
but paired. Her diary was open on the table,
the phonetic scrawl reading,
Is ther a Gad? I do not no.
Ons apon a tyme
the king had a dahter. *Wat a beutee she waz,*
her hart like a roze petal faling,
and I knew she would find a language
to hold what I could not.

5.

It doesn't help when you ask me
about it, she told me calmly.
It helps when you know.
But it was not easy to find the right distance
to stand apart from her
when she taught me the clapping rhymes,
her right hand slapping my left
and then back to her own
before crossing again. We chanted
the barely disguised obscenities
that ended each stanza, that teasing lilt
girls learn in the schoolyard. *Oh mom,*
not like that, she scolded.
I thought I was doing
as I had been told. But she was teaching me
to bear my uselessness
and not turn away.

6.

We walked along the creekbed,
a fine linger of grass repeating
what had once been spilled
over the black, startled mud.
I squatted beside her
as she poked in sticks,
dug up handfuls of the wet dirt,
patted up a dam and kneaded it back down.
She began to hum, the music coming
first from her churning hands,
and then, slowly, from her lips
slipping apart.
Looking just up the hill,
we saw the skeleton of a marsh hawk
laid out, each bone
pausing precisely before the next,
the wings thrown out like white dice, and flight
only a memory
to bind together each separate thing.

Indian Summer

The children run ahead, flushing starlings
into the vineyards, and between the thistles
in a creek we never knew was there,

water touches all the hidden stones,
repeats each sky, each willow tree,
carries so much of what has happened
past these quiet boxes of hay
drying in the fields.

Soon the coming dark
will milk light from clouds.
A fisherman tosses back a silvered trout,
pausing before he casts again.
Deep in the undoing
of what the world has already done,

the shortening days
wheel their heat more gently over this valley,
and every chance
is a room to which we must return. Now the children

are chasing each other,
laughing as dust smokes around their shoes.
Our youngest lifts her shirt,
places my hand against a sharp wash of ribs.
Can you feel it? she whispers.

I cup the knocking from deep inside, so much
asking to be brought close
before it can be heard.

El Niño

Now the sky is tender,
the stone heart of these hills
glistening in sun.
It's four p.m. on Thursday,
the children eating cereal in the kitchen,
spoons chiming against their bowls.

Last night, I combed their hair outside,
listening to thunder, and then the silence
that begins a storm.

The older girls jumped the stoop
in nightgowns, their arms held out,
asking *Did I fly this time?*

I held the youngest on my lap,
my palm steadying her damp head,

thinking about rain in August,
the tradewinds hushed,
and somewhere on the equator
a pouring towards the empty side.

Each time I looked up,
silver leapt from darkness,
as water fell through light.

And it seemed then
I had been a long time
coming to this –

a moment of poise,

the force of a world
giving exactly what it takes away,

something close to rising
unfolding in my hand.

Salmon Run on the Consumnes River

Muscled black, their yearning
confuses the river's mouth.
One begins a volley of frantic jumps
up the ladder, and hundreds follow,
a slap as each salmon falls.
And here on shore,
a crowd of people press hard
against the chain-link fence.
A woman turns sideways
to make room for us, grey hair
barely contained in a barrette.
She smiles, then brushes a hand
against my youngest child's cheek,
against this wild longing
to draw close and closer still.
It is late in a November afternoon,
every face stung pink with cold,
same color of the sweater
my grandmother crumbled into my arms,
the last time I saw her, blind,
asking my name over and over,
her sad question like a snag
against whatever current pulls us on.
Downstream, black fins cut the water in looping eights.
We climb over quartz and granite,
and from where we sit, finally,
I can see torrents rushing through the weir,
and salmon struggling inside every swell,
the way that woman's tenderness
knocked me, for a moment, somewhere
between the two worlds we live within.
Above us, cormorants perch the wires,
while upstream, fishermen stand knee-deep in water,
lines cast out. In the failing light,
a salmon leaps through the river's slate,
edges broken gold, a brilliant ravine
drawn out, just barely,
before darkness churns back in.

Migration

Take this morning,
strained light of November,
clouds touching elm.

Take these colors
slowly dying back to gold.

What is winter
if not the heart before faith,
a history of summers
weeping alone, the rinsed sweetness
of reprieve
after you first come through grief?

Now,
take the certain arrow of these geese
flying down the delta
and moments later, this lone bird
crying for her flock.

Imagine how she listens for answer.
Imagine migration
as the longing we carry,

as a last call
to wings still folded inside.

Take heart.
Even if we never fly,
even if we are only falling,
we are not lost or left behind.

IV

At the Oyster Company Camp

Shoregrasses quiver, whispered seeds
twisting against chaff. Outside the storefront,
a young man in waders braids his black hair.
And inside the driftwood shacks,
women drill stringholes into shells,
men seed oysters,
children toss the threaded lines out to water.

It is not only the dead
who leave behind mysteries of bone,
tribal words for sleep and love, the years
falling like deadwood through a Bishop pine.

It is how the world asks to be spoken,
pennyroyal snowing blue across a ditch,
an osprey shadowing the buoyed dents,
this wind trying to tap each branch into life.
And yet, what happens to all that won't be heard,
to the listening that turns back to sorrow?

Soon the second tide will rinse over Estero bay
like all the longing
that cannot find a way into voice,

and all that can:
the bristled scraping of an old woman's broom
as she sweeps almost fifty years into mounds,
the late afternoon that returns a harvest of boats,
flocks of loons
lifting in a silver rush of wings,

the slow hush of fog
that closes this inlet throat of sky.

The Instructions

Sun flickers through your window,
the kitchen dark and moody with this storm.
You are explaining the physics of a rainbow,
your hands parted over a teapot
painted with two monks in prayer,
and these cups you made, long ago,
etched with galaxies and serpentine curves.
Draw a thread through the center of your eye,
you begin, and I cannot stop thinking
someone will be left with these cups,
and if it is me, they will be all I have
of my nipples taut inside your hands,
just once, my body as the compass point
and these circles of longing
bent by the entire spectrum
of what remains unsaid. I can almost feel
the searing heat of the sun unblanketed,
your tiny yard glistening after rain,
your back to me, now, as you fill the kettle.
If physics is a pattern for the infinite,
fragile and crudely marked,
tell me, what cruel miscalculation
gives us back memory instead,
how it relies on the angle of your shoulders
turned ninety degrees to the stove,
your voice a sightline
strung briefly between our lives,
so that whatever of the world streams in
settles too deep to touch.
You are saying
how much we see of beauty
depends wholly on where we rest,
but I don't know
how a mind could ever lose
this moment's stamp, your wrist
dragging blue sparks from a match,
tea cooling, already too cold to drink,
stone of this cup still warm, and embedded there,
instructions for holding on so long.

After reading that you have died,

I am alone, watching hours of chill
press a herringbone over the lake.
The sun has chosen
one ridge to change with light, and the water
answers in obsidian and coal.

Now you know so much more than I do
about listening, the way wind enters
where a jackrabbit bounds out from pines,
or how ice struggles to sheet this water
until shore is a hard line of longing.

You understand now, too,
that the unspoken gathers weight as we go,
the snow swallowing stump and print,
and history loses us, forgets the details
of summer, the lupine or startled birch
scattered deep into the forest.

Once you knew so much about sadness.

Maybe you sat on a bench like this,
blotting out the bleached scars
with your fingers, watching a skate of mist
nest between water and air, a moment of calm
before restlessness came seeping back in.

But now, you are stillness
that has never been torn open. A stone
travelling easily in hand. The carrying
without wanting to be set down.

— in memory of K.K., 1958 - 1994

Fidelity

A dove burst up through the wild grass,
her flapping so close I felt a brief shudder
parting air, asking what in me still remembered to fly,
and for that moment I was launched,
a star piercing the sadness
the world had carried for so long. I wanted to leave you.
I wanted to leave everywhere
water slipped unseen into distance,
the fields rattling with seed, the rust of noon
hazing the sloughs. But loving best
what is just beyond reach
is a dying too,
even if I feel only a small gnawing
further in than I can touch; even if my youngest child
asks me to look into the untouched blue
at the center of every sky.

Still, it is hard not to see
that we have changed. After dinner in our yard,
I look at your arms, your hands, at the weight
of all that needs us to hold back.
Our daughters crawl through a break in the hedge,
chalking letters on the neighbor's sidewalk,
and their bodies are nutted hard
with what begins dark and wonderful.
I wish you had found me at nineteen,
but another man worked in that orchard with me,
the buzzing thick with heat.
And because the flesh
has its own momentum apart from love,
first we softened, the ripeness that spreads from the knotting
and unknotting all at once; and then, afterward,
I followed him into the cold steel of the walk-in,
squatting between splintered crates,
pinching the luminous buttocks of each apricot
and ate the sweetest fruit,
tiny rivers of juice glistening, dark pebbles of stain
falling down around me. Memory

does not move us in accidental ways.
When you push aside a plate to touch me,
a paper napkin flutters to grass,
and I remember that sudden bird
as a flint striking mercy; and the instant of rushing-in
she left behind, as my soul beginning
to stay close by the emptiness
I cannot fill with another,

saying *You do not have to lose everything
to know what has landed deep inside.*

Counting As She Does In Summer

We sit on the river dock
and I listen to her love the numbers.
I want to count as she does,
all rhythm and no burden, each sound
not yet fastened to what comes next.
It is already August. Behind me,
I recall the tune of dimes in my pocket
as we ran after the ice cream truck,
and a wealth of starch
whispering from the clothesline. And last night,

as she slept in the house,
her window dimly lit, her dreaming
lulled by the lamp's earnest silence,
I lay outside, naming stars.
For a moment, then, I felt a wordless river
counting me across to another shore, and there,
I moved so easy and unencumbered
that the fire in me came to water,
and the water in me reached into something else.

Now, gnats tangle the greying heat.
Holding her on my lap, I strain forward
so she can slip her hand
through the dark tension of water.
I imagine walking through that field
on the distant bank, and resting there,
the shape of my weight
printed in timothy grass. But I cannot carry her
safely through the current,
and how could I leave her behind,
frantic to turn the river aside?

I remember the story a lover told me once
about an entomologist who breathed
in a chemical so that he forever became
a candle of scent for gypsy moths.
And because the moths were drawn to him,
waiting in clusters at every door and window,

and because they pulsed their dusted wings
around him standing in the dark,

he understood what a woman does about love:
the body helpless
against what opens through her,
the body lost and given over
to the larger need of whatever comes next.

Deadlock

Because sometimes a place enters more easily than desire,
we drive down to where the river darkens.
Centuries of oaks stand still as patience,
bats wildly erasing blackness in disappearing silver lives.
As we skip rocks across the glassy surface,
Venus swells into view.
    If only language could leap like this
across our separate lives, shadows arcing,
bouncing, the touch down
so utterly forgiving. But each stone still in your hand
has a weight equal to all we cannot find a way to speak.
What does water know,
resisting rock, yet slipping open for this heron
diving into minnows?
    And where are the words to keep you
from turning back to the car, to this month of swallowed curses
sparking like the tattered fires along the road's edge?
Here in the valley, rice farmers drop a match into their fields,
flames rinsing the stubble
of whatever chaos spring has left behind.
How much harder to work the heart clean

when silence has its own country,
wild with power, driving tires over highway, past my last chance
to tell you, *Stop, turn back, unclothed*
you can still take me
falling into dark water.

Watching Hale-Bopp with an Old Friend

— for Gregory

Under stars thrown in white dust
and the comet's crescent burn,
you talk about neutrinos,
particles so small
they hurtle through our bodies,
touching nothing, so many of them,
that I imagine myself floating apart,
beginning my smoky rise into sky.

A headlight parts the vineyard as it passes,
and in the darkness taking us back,
you tell me your brother
writes from prison – *Nine years*
for entering the house of a sleeping friend,
and sure I was drunk,
but its worse than that,
tell me, how could her terror
have felt so much like love?

I picture him in his cell,
neutrinos moving as pure velocity
through his orange shirt and pants,
his grey blanket, a steel sink,
untouched by gravity,
unpulled by human longing
or the searing orbit of his shame.

You set your telescope into velvet,
click the metal latches down.
I hold you then, your shoulder blades
like wings in my palms. Each collision
brings danger, the way we live
half our lives like this, brief moments
of coming only so close,

and then apart,
this dirt road rising like starlight
in the swirl of dust behind my car, and you
alone in that field, looking up at every world
on its way to somewhere else.

After despair

and months of listening
to the dying acres

click sheaf to sheaf,
we ride our bicycles

inside the irrigated fields. Here
a man fishes the ravine,

his strung catch
floating in a bucket.

And when our children ask
if they can touch the carp,

meaning the bulging eyes,
the barbed scales,

the violence of a generous world
seeding itself over and over,

he tells them,
Touch all you can.

Small wonder,
a morning in this heat

seems a delicate skein
tied between faith and risk,

when small rooms
are opening in the alfalfa

as blackbirds fly up
from hidden sloughs,

their wings dipped
and sparking red.

What if devotion
is the smallest moment

we can enter,
and these birds

are slipping in and out
as if to make the portal wide?

How much is given,
and how easily

it must be lost,
if hope glistens like this –

not the sudden plume of darkness
fired into sun,

but rolling off the wetted feathers,
water,

fine as smoke,
spinning down behind.

Stillwater Cove

Sea booms faintly through the open windows,
and all through the long glaze of afternoon,
I am trying to remember
words to a song, but melody spills everywhere:
children wheeling through salt grass,
a young buck beginning horns
who startles at our daughters
digging with spoons for fieldmice,
the baby waking from her nap, who calls me to her,
her skin smelling like wind, musky with water,
the sea figs redding into embers
the sky seeming to open and dip to the coastline,
the grammar of time broken down,
and thrown further from the center of each day.

I bathe the children in the sink, a hover of soap
lighting on their hair,
and in the beginning dark,
we trace Scorpio's crooked tail of light.
How vast the sky
lost of horizon, lost of the lyrics that orient us
to the map of music, but not the music itself.
Below us, tides are pulling silver water
away from mollusks and anemones,
uncovering crabs scuttling across the rocks.
And here, the fog begins
climbing the fields,
erasing the roofline and walls of this house,
until there is nothing left to steer by
but the lamp blurring our nightstand,
the slight rattle of pages
as wind fingers our forgotten books, and your hands
singing what the words will never know.

In the Tidal Fields

I hover just outside the back door
opening from the children's room into Tomales bay,
waiting as I often do
to hear their stories ease the dark,
waiting for the utter yes
of their bodies to slow and twine.
Earlier this evening, I watched them running
over a sparse comb of plantain.
A flock of bank swallows shuddered white,
and then turning, poured into a grey thimble
before scattering apart.
Our youngest asked me, *Will those birds be dead too?*
while the cupped wings of her palms lifted and fell,
and it seemed her hands already knew.

Now the pasture sleeps in water,
mollusks spilling through the black estero
like stars opening in a cold sky.
Remember when you first told me
every star in our galaxy was rushing away
from the same beginning into nowhere.
It hurt to imagine an infinite absence
and no returning home.
Tell me, I said, *if the sky is a vast memory,*
how can we become nothing again?
That was before you almost died.

Strange, then, each night,
how I grow more certain
all we love gathers a gravity within,
and our lives will not forget us,
but will become dense with longing
until the parchment of the body ignites,
throwing a wheel of radiant shadow
outside this world and finally, we will fly,
weightless and everywhere at once.

At the Vernal Pools

April, and the prairie is splintered with light.
While sheep graze these repaired pastures,
and blackbirds trill out territories, ghosts of the first settlers

are homesteading untried grasslands, losing children
to unnamed fevers, surrendering to the infinite
helplessness in farming lands that are always returning

from drought or flood. Now you spread a blanket
over sedge fattened on enormous months of rain,
so we can set out strawberries and wine.

I o the baby's newly furred head,
so gluttonous with life, thinking of her sisters' lengths
inching up the yardstick you nailed to a door,

both so impatient to arrive where we finally are:
here, in the midst of this brief flowering of the vernal pools.
We have been waiting years for enough storms

to coax rings of wildflowers around the journey
of this lake gathering itself back into clay.
Waiting without knowing what else we would be given:

great herons floating out over the marsh, egrets startling
into white arrows, and the blue shadow of Mount Diablo
anchoring us to this salted horizon.

When I no longer wanted to die,

and was not working back to my father
as he hurled a shuffle of volumes
down the table, madly cracking spines
of Britannica and Asia, so that I had to stare
too hard into the lilac
festering with wasps outside our window;

or even further back to my great-grandfather
nimbly cinching a slipknot for his throat,
cornhusks soaked in vodka and the Jersey cow
butted up against her stall, my grandfather
dragging the hated limpness of his father
away from the barn as it surrendered to fire;

I did not understand that I was returning
to the first time my mother lowered
the new weight of my sister
into my lap and I held on
to all that could be; to the night
I willed my body through the cold lake

into moon, that water bony with light;
or even after my father slammed
out the screen door, how I quietly taped
across the ripped muzzle of a brown bear,
restoring the bookjacket of a river
throttled with salmon. I only knew

that something wanted to keep on
falling through the late summer dusk,
down the Sierras, granite and fir
suddenly opening into barley fields
spindled with dust, floodways gathering
live oaks into the drying loam;

that days apart from you
had brought me down the mountains
to where the longing to be gone
had become this impatience to arrive,
all the wind through my windows
whispering *This is where we live.*

Blue Moon

There is a lost gull
disappearing over the whispered rows of corn.
All summer, I longed to walk
inside the sheltered dark of those fields,
as if the girl that I was
waited there with a knife and whiskey,
wishing God was a seabird
to carry her back through water.

You did not know me then,
or how I stood on a washed out pier,
struggling with that last step into air,
watching gulls spindle over the sunken braces,
their white sails like stitches
hastened into sky.

And tonight, the moon twice ripe
in a single month,
sweetness stains dark as any grief. Perhaps
this is a little of what you love in me,
how the soul enlarges in these wanted hours,

having traveled through the kind of hurt
which changes everything,

having turned from a sea that cannot sleep
into this heat
blown through with crows. We sit on the porch,

listening to wind swell the corn,
to the rustle of husks
that almost sounds like rain.
Torn shadow.
The world enters through a wound.
Somewhere in this blackness, moonlight
returns the riverbed to glistening,
and the only water in this valley
dreams of going deeper in.

Windstorm on the Marsh

We lie beside the drowning grass,
willows groaning

as they are torn apart,
tire tracks

swept clean of dust
and lifted up like bones.

It's hard, love, always
coming into something else,

and this is how we'll go,
isn't it,

back to where the geese
drag beneath this sky,

the loons
pulled down to silence,

a wordless rushing
over water.

Back to where the pintails
thrown up in flocks,

are thrown back in pairs.
How hard they work

to splint their wings
against the gusts, and still

the ducks are dropping
in a wild salt of dark,

in the mated hands of God
that will break us

back to one.
Hardest,

where I love you most,
how we touch

beneath the emptied lanterns
of the rushes

and watch the shaken sky.

Recent Books
from Anhinga Press

Three-legged Dog
Donald Caswell, 1999

Woman and the Sea, Selected Poems
Michael Mott, 1999

Braid
Mia Leonin, 1999

*Runaway with Words: A Short Course on Poetry
and How to Take It with You*
Joann Gardner, 1998

*Runaway with Words: A Collection of Poems
from Florida's Youth Shelters*
Edited and Introduced by Joann Gardner, 1997

The Secret History of Water
Silvia Curbelo, 1997

This Once
Nick Bozanic, 1997

Walking Back from Woodstock
Earl S. Braggs, 1997

Hello Stranger: Beach Poems
Robert Dana, 1996

*Isle of Flowers:
Poems by Florida's Individual Artist Fellows*
Donna J. Long, Helen Pruitt Wallace, Rick Campbell, eds., 1995

*Unspeakable Strangers:
Descents into the Dark Self, Ascent into the Light*
Van K. Brock, 1995

The Secret Life of Moles
P. V. LeForge, 1992

North of Wakulla: An Anthology
M. J. Ryals and D. Decker, eds., 1988

The Anhinga Prize
for Poetry Series

Out of print

About the Author

Julia B. Levine's recent awards in poetry include The Discovery/The Nation Award, the Pablo Neruda Prize in Poetry, an Americas Review Award, the Lullwater Review Prize in Poetry, and a fellowship from the California Arts Council. Her poems have appeared in or are forthcoming in *The Lullwater Review, The Southern Poetry Review, The Nation, Prairie Schooner, Nimrod,* and *Zone 3.*

Julia Levine received her Ph.D in Clinical Psychology from the University of California, Berkeley. She works in Davis, California where she lives with her three small children and her husband.

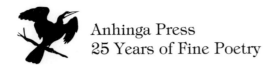

Anhinga Press
25 Years of Fine Poetry

Anhinga Press is pleased, and not a little shocked, to be celebrating its 25th anniversary in 1999. Any small press that lives for 25 years is doing something right. A small press that lives on poetry alone, as Anhinga has, is performing a miracle. Because we are happy to be doing as well as we are doing, we want to celebrate our birthday and poetry too.

Anhinga Press owes its longevity and its measure of success to a handful of hard-working people dedicated to publishing good poetry. Van Brock, Don Caswell, Julie Weiler, Mary Jane Ryals, P.V. LeForge, Lynne Knight and a few others have worked hard through the years to make Anhinga what it is.

And, even more importantly, the poets that Anhinga has published have worked to promote and sell their books. Without their efforts, we would have books in warehouses and not in readers' hands. Finally, without the aid of the Florida Division of Cultural Affairs and the Florida Arts Council, Anhinga Press would not have enjoyed its recent success.

We are looking toward the future now. Another 25 years? Who knows? More good poems that tell us something about living in the world? Yes. That's a simple, but important enough goal to take with us into the new year, the new millennium. Springsteen says, "At the end of every hard-earned day, people find some reason to believe." Here, we've found one of ours.

— *Rick Campbell*
Director, Anhinga Press
1999